A Joke Book for Kids

Clean Jokes for Kids

Written and Illustrated by Jerry Harwood

www.AJokeBookForKids.com

INFI∞ITY
PUBLISHING

Copyright © 2010 by Jerry Harwood
Cover design by Jerry Harwood

ISBN 0-7414-5926-4

Printed in the United States of America

Published March 2010

INFINITY PUBLISHING
1094 New DeHaven Street, Suite 100
West Conshohocken, PA 19428-2713
Toll-free (877) BUY BOOK
Local Phone (610) 941-9999
Fax (610) 941-9959
Info@buybooksontheweb.com
www.buybooksontheweb.com

To all children who are eager to learn, and eager enjoy funny and important things that happen around them as they journey toward adulthood. I would also like to give special recognition to the inspirational children, parents, and staff at St. Paul School in Florence, Kentucky.

FOREWORD

Jerry Harwood has been a teacher and bus driver for over 37 years. Throughout his career he has amassed many jokes given to him by his students. This book is a collection of jokes and humor about school, school life, teachers, and lessons in life that have helped Jerry provide some levity in driving and teaching over the years. Some jokes are great and some are blunders, but they are the best that kids have provided as the years have come and gone to make each day _extra_-ordinary.

Sit back, enjoy and be ready to laugh or groan, but remember one of life's great treasures – *"a little laughter brightens the day"*.

Randy Poe
Superintendent
Boone County Schools

What do you call a bird that is always getting hurt? Ow! (owl).

When Bert asked his friend for ice cream, what did his friend say? "Sher-bert."

Why didn't the road crew let the duck cross the road? Because they didn't want a "quack" in the "woad."

According to the chicken, the most dangerous bird watcher is... the Red-tailed chicken hawk.

What do you call an adult who sucks his thumb?
A big baby.

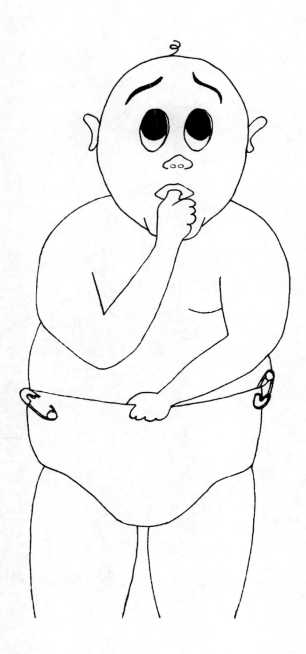

What do you call a bell that's a little crazy? A Ding-a-ling.

Why did the deputy sheriff show up at the kindergarten class?
Because he heard there was a kid-knapping.

Why was the kid named Burt, happy everyday?
Because he was always having a Burt-day.

**How do you know that an alligator that always
eats at the deli, would be a good manager?
Because he's a good deli-gator.**

**What do you call a gator that lives on narrow streets
between buildings in the city? An alley- gator.**

What do you call funny music that's written especially for automobiles? Car-tunes.

Where did they send the car after the accident so it could regain its looks and have a good time? To the Wreck-Creation-center.

Why did the dog have a booth at the flea market?
He wanted to get rid of some used fleas.

Where did the dog get his fleas?
At the flea market.

**How many birds does it take to clean
a birdcage? Toucan!**

**A chicken was on vacation. He arrived at his hotel. He
walked up to the front desk, and the desk clerk said:
"Are you here to <u>CHECK-IN</u> <u>CHICK-EN</u>?"**

A backpack was in a race with a ball cap. For a while, the cap went on a-head, but finally the backpack won. Why, because the backpack was zippier.

What did the backpack say to the kid?
I've got your back.

Why can't the minister communicate with the garbage can? Because the garbage can only understands trash talk, and the minister never talks trash.

Just because the big kids pick on you, doesn't necessarily mean you're a little booger.

What do you call an extremely good nickel that disappears after it delivers gifts to all the children? Saint Nickel-less.

**What kind of boyfriend does a girl monkey prefer?
A hunky monkey.**

What kind of parties do monkeys have at the zoo?
Parties where they can eat, drink, and be hairy.

Why do so many people think monkeys are crazy?
Because monkeys are always going bananas.

Why does a hot dog always feel great after a race?
Because he's always the Wiener.

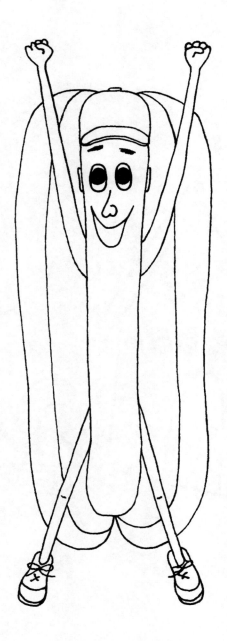

What did the redneck say to the hotdog that won the race?
You're the wiener!!!

What do you say when your dog runs away?
Dog Gone!

What did the good-looking fire hose say to the burning, hot fire?
Do you want to go out tonight?

**What kind of movies do chickens like?
Chick flicks.**

What did the mother hen say to her little chick that was complaining? I don't want to hear another "peep' out of you.

There was a racing, greyhound dog, named "Grand Larceny."
At the last minute, he was scratched. When they
found him, he was back in the pen.

What trees love to be petted?
A Dogwood, and a Pussy Willow.

If a bee drove a school bus, what would his job title bee? A "Buzzzz" Driver.

What do you call a bee that has a very possessive girlfriend? Her-bee.

After the jail work-detail had gone back to the jail for the night, Manny, who had fallen asleep in the truck on the way back, discovered that he had been accidentally left out. This immediately brought back bad, old memories of when he was left out of things during his childhood, but for some reason, this time, he wasn't really upset.

What did the old lady decide to do, to
look younger? Diet and Dye it.

The snowman family was at home, when the doorbell rang. Mr. Snowman went over to the door and said, "Who is it?"
The answer came back, "It's snow buddy."

Why was the ice cube afraid to go into the dairy bar freezer?
Because he heard they make ice "scream" in there.

What did the cookie say to the un-greased cookie pan? I'm stuck on you.

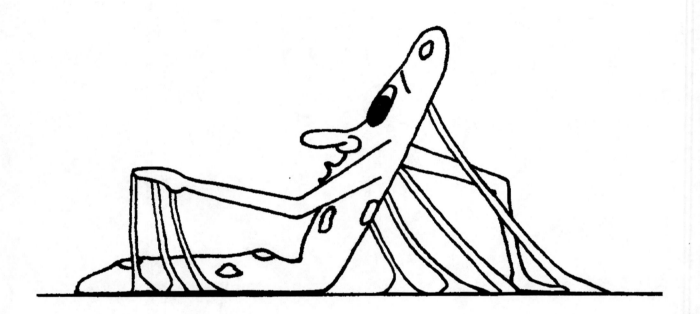

On a school bus, more than one person can sit in a seat, unless her name is "Phyllis Seet."

**What do you call a group of nice honeybees?
A honey bunch.**

**When a bee landed on a pretty flower, what did he say to the
Sun? Thanks for making all these pretty flowers so hot.**

What do you say when one of your bananas jumps out of your bunch, and runs away? A banana's split.

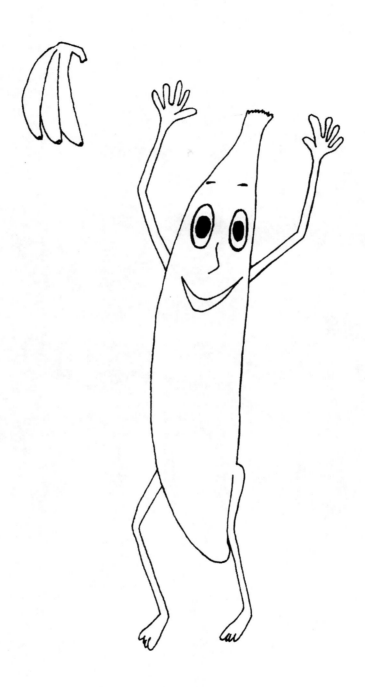

What do you call a fly that falls into the butter dish? A butter-ed fly.

The place books are kept to loan out is a library, pronounced lie-brair-ee. Some people pronounce it lie-berry, which is incorrect.

You are really good looking!

What is a lie-berry? A. A lie berry is a large, red, juicy, and delicious berry that grows in the southern states. If you eat these berries, you will lie for 24 hours. Hopefully there will be no lasting side effects from such a mistake.

Why was the girl named Dee so busy?
A. Because her name had so much meaning. My-dee, tie-dee, miss-dee, hi-dee, fri-dee, speed-dee, me-dee, I-dee, bye-dee, a-dee, b-dee, c-dee, e-dee, k-dee, L-dee, m-dee, o-dee, p-dee, q-dee, r-dee, y-dee, z-dee, we-dee, dye-dee, bed-dee, gree-dee, lay-dee, hay-dee, may-dee, ted-dee, red-dee, swee-dee, can-dee, bald-dee, tweed-dee, bod-dee, god-dee, cad-dee, dad-dee, fad-dee, had-dee, lad-dee, mad-dee, pad-dee.

How-Dee!

What did the minister say to Faith's Mom before Faith was born? You've got to have "Faith."

How do you know it's no fun to work for a school system? Because all school employees are bored - (board) employees.

Why did the little boy not like school? Because he was just a little board – (bored).

**Why did the little rabbit always make people laugh?
Because he was a funny bunny.**

**What did the hungry kitty cat say to the chubby little bunny?
Hi hare ball.**

A basketball player went to the doctor for a flu shot, but the doctor was out of flu shots. What did the basketball player say? Since you're out of flu shots today, when I come back, do I get a "free shot?"

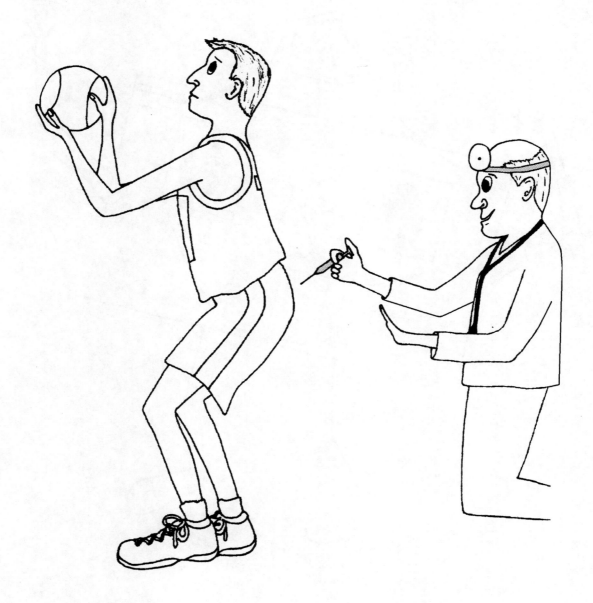

When the nose wanted to get on the basketball team, what did he say to the coach? Pick me, pick me!

Have you ever seen a school "dance"?

What monster likes to dance?
The boogieman, he likes to boogie.

What do you get when you cross a frog with a bull?
A Bullfrog.

What is a frog's favorite year? Leap year.

What did the snow lady say when the snowman asked her to marry him? "Snow way."

What did the boy volcano say to his erupting girlfriend? You're Hot! "I Lava you."

What is the warmest and friendliest Fish?
The cuttlefish.

Where does a tired fish sleep? In a waterbed.

**Even though the seamstress did only so-so work,
it seems, that she already had the job sewn up.**

**What two body parts remind you
of a flower? Two-lips.**

**What do you call it when two convicts
get married? Con-fusion.**

**What do you call food fried by your
little sister? Sissy-fried.**

What do you scream to your cousin Billy when he's flying your plane too close to the ground in Kentucky?
A-h-h-h-h, Hill! Billy! Lookout!

What do you say to a guy who's trying to take your airplane away from you? Hi Jack!

**What did the newly married bee bride say to her new husband?
"This is our honeymoon, honeybee."**

**What does a lady bee use to fix her hair
in the morning? A honeycomb.**

What do you say to a cookie that win's the spelling bee? "You're a smart cookie."

What's your prediction for the weather this winter? I see, Icee!

What did the snow ladies say when they checked in at their diet workshop? "We've lost snow weight."

There was a little boy named Sho. You may say "Sho what," When you know his last name, you'll know where he's from. He's from the south, Sho-nuff.

What do you say about a snowman that's not very nice? He might be able to <u>make</u> a snow angel, but "He's" snow angel!!

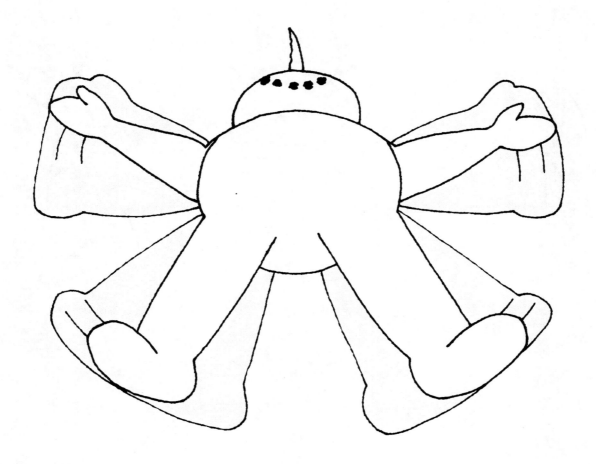

**What smart-elick tree always talks back?
The Sassy Frass. (Sassafras)**

What do you call a dog that has to spend the winter outside? A chilly dog.

What do you say about a cold and snowy winter day with no jokes? It's snow fun.

What do you call someone who's always crushing caterpillars? A caterpillar killer.

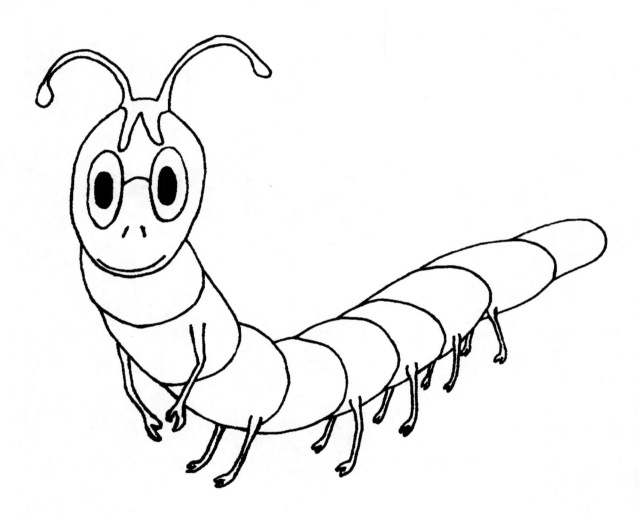

What do you call a formal dance held for the basket company employees? A Basket Ball.

Ali Gator and her family love to play softball, because an alligator family makes a great team.

Does putting butter on your popcorn make it better?
"You Butter believe it."

What does a school bus with no tires need?
It needs to be re-tired.

How do you know School Bus Drivers are strong?
They can pick up a busload of kids all by themselves.

What do you call a young man who likes to trick his girlfriend? Con-her – (Connor).

What do you call a boy who is always using his automatic camera? Camer-on – (Cameron).

**Why wouldn't the insurance company cover the "safe" driver?
Because they only cover people who drive cars.**

**Why couldn't the cowboy take his rope to church?
Because it was too knotty – (naughty).**

What is a Daffy – Dill?
It's not a flower; it's a funny pickle.

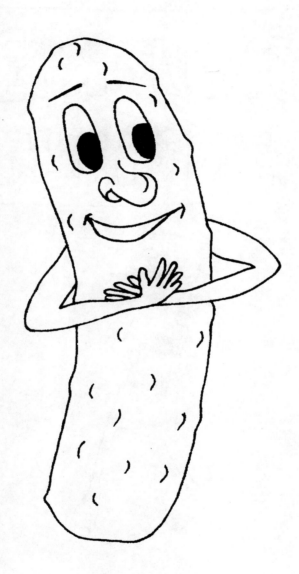

How do you make a pickle laugh?
You tickle a pickle.

Have you heard about the new grocery store where all the employees are frogs? They call it "Croak-ers."

What did the frog say about how deep the water was in his pond? Knee-deep – Knee-deep – Knee-deep.

Why was the kitty cat arrested? Because they discovered he was a "cat burglar."

What did the dog say when the kitty cat told him a cat joke? Are you kitty-ing me?

Why did the karate champion refuse to admit he had lost the karate competition? Because he was Pigheaded.

**Why did the bread man lose his job?
Because he was always loafing.**

What is a hippie's favorite vegetable? Peas, Baby.

This is a great knock-knock joke for a group of loud and rowdy kids. "Knock - knock – Who's there? Knock – knock it off!"

**On what day is a girl's boyfriend the nicest?
On Valentine's Day – on that day he's all heart.**

**What did the boy say to the good-looking
credit card? I get a charge out of you.**

Does this bow make me look fat?

What would you say about a snow girl who's always saying bad words? She's snow lady.

What did the E say after A helped him with his homework? "A," said E, "I. O. U." – (I owe you.)

What do you call a train that's out of control?
A "loco-motive."

What did the turkey say when he found himself in the oven? "I think it's a little stuffy in here."

**What did the turkey's girlfriend say to him?
You're looking perky turkey.**

Why were fish caught in the kitty- litter- box?
Because they were "cat"- fish.

What do you call a young person who is
learning to snorkel? A student diver.

What do you call Mr. and Mrs. Potato's three children? Tater tots.

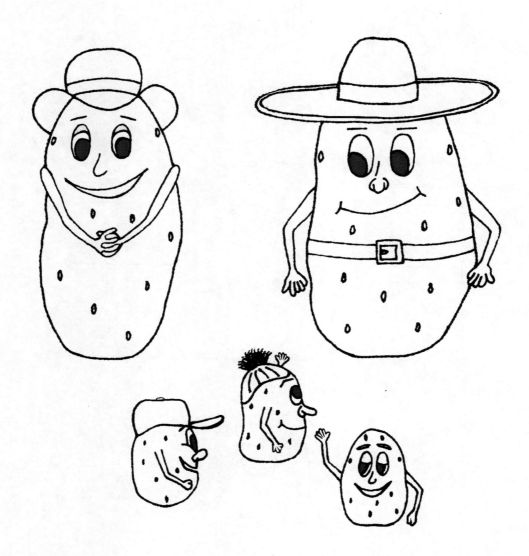

**Why couldn't the potato take a joke?
He was thin skinned.**

Why did Santa Claus cross the road?
To get to the other sleigh.

Little Caitlyn told her friend, "My Mommy got stopped by a policeman, and he gave her a ticket." Her little friend, Macy asked, "Was it a ticket to the movies?"

Why did the chicken have trouble crossing the road? Because one of her fans was in the way.

The teacher asked the little boy, "What are you going to be when you grow up?" The little boy said, "When I grow up, I'm going to be a booger, and that's snot funny, because everyone will pick on me.

What language do chickens and ducks speak? Fowl language.

What team sport reminds you of a cheer at a female boxing match? Soccer! – (Sock her).

What kind of music do they play at the gravel pit? Rock and Roll.

What kind of music do they play at the prison stone quarry? Hard rock.

**What is one of the most exciting times at the Zoo?
When the flamingoes dance the flamenco.**

**What did the overgrown tree say to
the tree trimmer? "Leaf me alone."**

What insect takes over when a thunderstorm causes the lights to go out? A lightning bug.

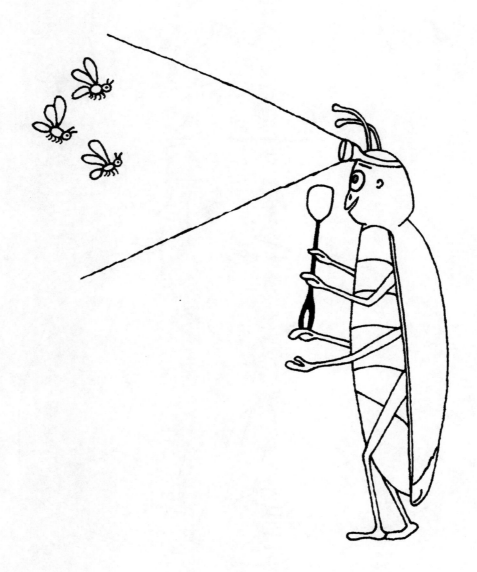

As the cute little Tomato and her friend, the Ball Cap, were running to the school bus stop, she remembered that she had forgotten something. So, she told the Ball Cap to go on a-head, and She would ketch-up later.

Does Santa like wrap music? Yes, He "Wraps" presents while listening to "Jingle Bells."

I don't like rap music, but I do have a favorite wrapper. A candy wrapper.

What did the little piggy want to be when he grew-up?
He wanted to be the biggest pig around, so
he could "Hog" all the food.

What kind of person likes to work all night
baking bread and sweet rolls? A Dough-Nut.

What is the perfect name for a man who sells eye glasses? Seymour – (see more).

A crazy man at the seashore reminds you of what tree? A Beech-nut.

A couple dolphins were swimming really, really fast, and they ran into a school of sea bass. One of the sea bass said, "Hey, you ran into us." The dolphin said, "Not on porpoise!"

Around Easter, the Easter Bunny is a regular "basket case."

What did Santa Claus say to his deer friend, Rudolph, the red nosed reindeer? "Rudy, I think we're going to need you and your nose this Christmas."

What do you call a robot that's a homeless drifter? A Robo Hobo.

Mr. Snowman was trying to clean the snow from his driveway with a leaf rake, and he asked his friend why it was not working. His friend said, "Well, that's snow shovel."

What did the school bus driver say to the kids who were walking around in the school bus while it was moving? He said, "When the school bus is a-rollin' kids should not be a-strollin'."

Why did the chicken put her oldest egg into a time-out?
Because the rotten little egg was acting spoiled.

Why was the egg not laughing?
Because he didn't think the yokes were funny.

What did the little girl on the teeter-totter say to her heavy friend? You're not holding up your end.

Kids who tend to spit on people when they talk should stop using such juicy language.

Why did the female runner push her friend, Peng, over the finish line? Because she had always wanted to see a peng-win. (PENGUIN)

What do you hear when your oldest and smartest firecracker goes off? A Wisecrack.

For kids, news time is snooze time.

**Where would you most likely find a girl
named Paige? In a bookstore.**

What tree always has to see the tree doctor?
The Sycamore, it's always "sick-ah-more" than other trees.

What do you call a lion that's just average in school?
A (c)-lion (sea lion).

What did the rooster say to his new girlfriend?
You're a cute chick.

Why did the chicken cross the road?
Because all her chicken friends were egging her on.

**What did the young snowman-ice skater say to his
ice skating partner when she lost her balance?
Are you falling for me?**

**What did the doctor say about the little boy
with a runny nose? "He's - snot well."**

What did the child psychologist say about the kid with a runny nose? "The child has a tissue issue."

**Why did the booger cross the road?
I don't know, but it's snot funny.**

**How do you know that trucks are always tired?
They always carry their beds with them.**

**Did you hear about the school bus driver who was arrested
because he was driving while loaded? Yes, but it's not
against the law to drive a school bus loaded with kids.**

**Why did the egg refuse to listen to very funny jokes?
He was afraid he would crack-up.**

**What do you call your favorite ball cap that's always
available for you to use? A handy-cap.**

What did the minister say when the cow showed up at church? Holy cow!

What do you call a cow that lives in an air-conditioned barn? A real cool cow.

What flower is the silliest flower? The Daffy-Dill.

What did the guitar say to the musician?
You pick on me too much.

Why wouldn't the rooster fight the other rooster?
Because he was a big "chicken."

Why did the frog take a nerve pill?
Because he was feeling a little jumpy.

**What did the slow thinking bear say to the teacher
when he couldn't finish his math test on time?
Please bear with me.**

**When the little bear cub got a boo-boo, what advice
did his mom give him? Grin and bear it.**

What did Santa Claus say to the bad little boy who had a head cold? "If you want a present this Christmas, Don't be so naughty, snotty."

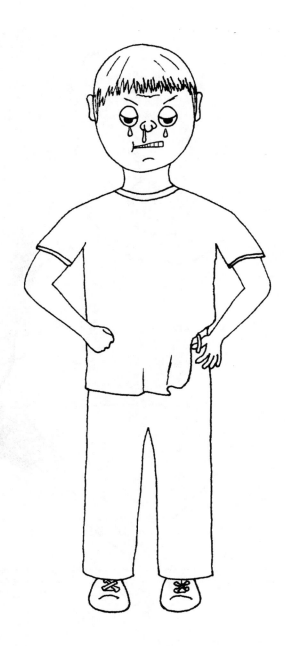

What do you call a crazy man and his girlfriend? Nut 'n Honey.

If you ever see a mouse in your house with cheese, whatever you do, don't give him a knife. Because, you don't want him to cut the cheese.

What did the little bee's mom do when she caught him doing something wrong? She spanked his "bee-hind."

Why was Mother Earth so proud of her Sun?
Because he was so bright.

What did the swimming pool say to his good friend, the Sun?
You give me a warm feeling.

**What did the girl-phone say to her friend
the boy phone? "Call me."**

**What did the stop sign say to the
no parking sign? Nice sign language.**

What vegetable doesn't pull its own weight? A dead-beet.

**What did the backpack say to its most talkative zipper?
"Zip it!"**

How did the state of Michigan get its name?
A truck driver named Gan and his wife lived in a northern
territory. Once, when he was about to leave on a long trip, his
wife said, I'll (Miss Ya Gan)" (Michigan).

The next year, the couple had a little girl and named her
after her Dad. What do you think they named her?
More-Gan (Morgan).

One dark morning a little Kindergarten girl was riding the School Bus, and asked the bus driver to turn the interior lights on so she could read her book. The bus driver explained to her that it was dangerous to keep the interior lights on while driving. At that time, an eighth grader from the back of the bus yelled, "God said, let there be light." "Then, a little Kindergarten boy from up front, replied, "Yes, but God meant, let there be light ---- Outside!"

What did the city council do when a steer escaped into the city streets from a wrecked cattle truck? They appointed a Steering Committee.

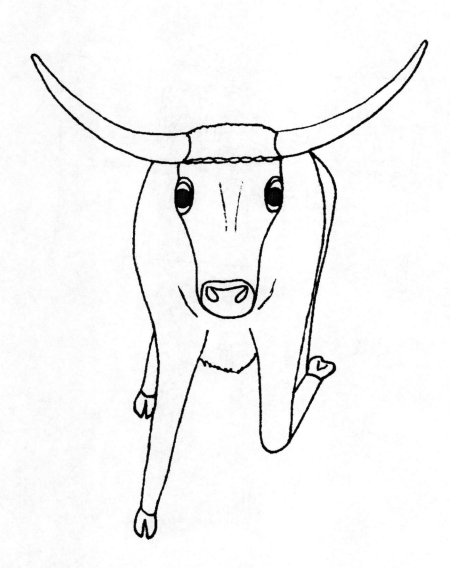

What do you get when you shine a spotlight on your bull? A Bull-lit.

How does it affect students when the first grade teacher has a "4 Sale Sign?" The kids will only be able to count like this, 1,2,3,5,6,7,8,9,10.... She sold all the 4's.

What season of the year is brought on by gravity? Fall

**Why was the tiny insect so nice?
Because, she was a ladybug.**

**Mr. and Mrs. Oculars had a baby boy who had extremely
fine vision. What do you think they named him? Ben
Ben Oculars – (Binoculars).**

**What does a Nuclear Scientist
like to do for fun? Go fission.**

**A turnip farmer called the police from the farmers market, and
told them all his vegetables were missing. They told him
not to worry. They would surely turn-up.**

What do you call a bird that is arrested and convicted of a crime? A jailbird.

Why didn't the little bird trust the tree? Because the tree was a little shady.

What do you call a waiter who has no weight? A ghost waiter.

What's a bull's favorite food? Bull-loney.

**What did the hotdog say to the little wiener dog?
Where's your bun, dog?**

**What happened to the librarian when a deputy sheriff
showed up at school? She was booked.**

What did the tapeworm want to do when he grew up? He wanted to measure-up.

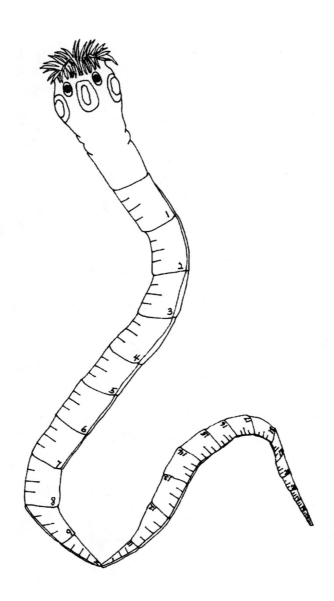

Why did the zookeeper rush to the man's house with the poorly kept lawn? He heard the man had a lot of dandy-lions (dandelions) in his yard, and the zoo needed a Dandy lion.